Your Haunted Lives

A Collection of Strange And Chilling True Tales

From The *My Haunted Life Too* Website

Edited by

G. Michael Vasey

For Paul, Liam, Jon and Denisa and visitors to My Haunted Life Too

Because, everyone has a story.....

Copyright ©2016 Asteroth's Books
All rights reserved

ISBN - **978-0-9961972-2-9**

Text copyright: G. Michael Vasey

All rights reserved. Except for brief quotations in critical articles or reviews, no part of this book may be reproduced in any manner without prior written permission from the editor.

The rights of G. Michael Vasey as editor have been asserted in accordance with the Copyright Designs and Patents Act 1988.

Contents

FOREWORD BY DARREN MARLAR — 10

INTRODUCTION — 14

MORE GHOSTS IN THE MACHINES... — 16

Voicemail — 16
A Voice From Beyond The Grave — 17
Creepy Christmas Cell Phone — 19
Weird Call — 20
The Dead Calling — 21
Patient Speaks on the Radio While in Surgery — **22**
The Intervening Daemon — 24
The Voice in the Wilderness — 25
My Driving Angel — 26

PROTECTIVE PRESENCES — 28

The Vigil — 28
Ghostly Angel? — 30
The Old Man in the Graveyard — 30
Near Death Experience — 32
Ghost Writer — 33
My Protective Grandmother — 34
Grandma's Ghost and the Babysitter — 35
Uncle's Last Visit — 37

HAUNTED PICTURES — 39

A Possessed Painting? — 40

OUIJA BOARD TROUBLES — 42

Ouija Board Ghost — 42
Never Abuse The Undead — 42

HAUNTED HOUSES — 44

A Haunted House — 44
The Ghost Who Locked Me Out of My House — 48
The Old Man — 50
Mr. Skeleton — 51
Lady in Black — 52
Boy in the Sailor Suit — 53
The Cigar Smoking Ghost — 55
A Haunted Barroom — 56
Window Watcher — 57
Invisible Ghost — 58
Unseen Presence in My Bedroom — 59
What Are You Going to Do? Shoot A Ghost? — 59
Crying Lady — 61
Albert — 62
Old Woman — 63
The Victorian House Basement — 64
A Ghostly Dog - A Scary Ghost Story — 66
The Haunted House in Detroit — 67
House Occupied.... — 68

HAUNTED LOCATIONS — 70

Something Dangerous in the Woods? — 70
The Boneyard — 71
A Ghostly Gas Station — 72
Haunted Military Location — 74

GHOSTS ON THE ROAD — 77

THE FACELESS GHOST	77
THE GHOST THAT DECLINED A LIFT	78
GHOSTLY CAR IN DETROIT	79
THE GHOSTLY HORSE RIDER	80
MY FIRST HAND EXPERIENCE OF THE CIVIL WAR	81
THE FARMER'S DAUGHTER	83

DEMONS AND EVIL SPIRITS — 86

GREEDO	86
GREEN DEMON?	88
A DEMON OF A PARTY	89
RED DEMON	90
THE DEMON IN MY DREAMS	91

JUST DOWNRIGHT BIZARRE — 93

SHARING A BED WITH A GHOST?	94
MY GIRLFRIEND'S GHASTLY FRIEND	95
THE CURSED SKULL	96
THE VISITOR FROM VIETNAM	97
BOY IN THE CLOSET	98
THE WITCHES' DAUGHTER	100
A JUMP THROUGH SPACE?	102
UNBORN CHILD	103
STRANGE HAPPENINGS IN NEW ENGLAND	105
THE GHOST THAT LOVED ME	106
THE GIRL IN THE MIRROR	107

ABOUT MY HAUNTED LIFE TOO WEBSITE

110

ABOUT G. MICHAEL VASEY — 111

OTHER BOOKS   **112**

OTHER POETRY COLLECTIONS   **113**

Foreword by Darren Marlar

I remember my first scare. It was in a book.

I've never been a fan of horror – on the screen, that is. For some unknown reason, God wired me in such a way that I just do not scare easily, so the films promoted as "terrifying" and "frightening" usually left me bored. As a child my friends would talk about films such as *Halloween*, *Friday the 13th*, and *The Omen*. None of which raised my hairs in the slightest.

My elementary school library was full of books about ghosts, monsters, and all things that go bump in the night. Unlike the films, the books actually did excite me – although they didn't frighten me. I remember pulling two or three books of short stories at a time from the library shelves and getting a somewhat concerned look from our school librarian, Mrs. Frump. Honestly, I don't remember her actual name, but the moniker of Mrs. Frump, in my opinion, describes her quite accurately. I'm sure as she placed her red ink-soaked rubber stamp on the card in the back of each book, she envisioned me years later in a dark alley pulling the innards out of a stray cat with a pair of pliers, or something of the sort. For my ten-year-old self, books were the gateway to another dimension – even more so than reruns of "The Twilight Zone" that claimed to do so on television. Books were a collaboration between the author's mind and my own. I'd read the words and a new world would form all around me. And that is when I finally received my first scare.

I cannot tell you the name of the book or the author. I do remember it was an anthology of short stories about monsters, ghosts, and unsolved mysteries. I came to a chapter about a large creature, flying in the darkness, chasing after a speeding car with two love-struck teenagers inside, scared out of their minds. They could see the red eyes behind the car gaining ground on giant wings, and then suddenly a thud on the roof of the car, before claws tore through the metal.
My young mind could feel the wind hitting the kids' faces as the car sped down the road with its windows open. I could hear the scraping on the roof, the crying of the girl. I could see the glowing red eyes contrasted against the blackness of the road behind the speeding vehicle, dust kicked up from the rear tires. I could see the road curving ahead in the car's headlights and the boyfriend behind the wheel desperately trying to maintain control of the car while simultaneously comforting his girlfriend

while in a state of panic himself.

It may have been presented to me in black and white print, but in my mind it was very real... and the Mothman of Point Pleasant, West Virginia has been my favorite cryptid ever since.

Dark stories are still what I gravitate towards even as an adult. Take a look at the audiobooks I've narrated and you'll see they far outnumber the rest. So, when I decided to create a YouTube series and podcast of short stories, it was no contest what genre would be chosen. And thus began "Weird Darkness". The first episode? The Mothman of Point Pleasant... of course.

Now I have the privilege of narrating numerous stories from authors and fans all around the world, both fiction and non-fiction... including several stories from the editor of this book, G. Michael Vasey. And now I'm writing the foreword to one of his books that as a child I would have likely taken from the shelf and immersed myself in. I don't know if Mrs. Frump is still working the school library at Blackbob Elementary School in Olathe, Kansas... but if she is, I truly do hope that she opens up this book, sees my name, and smiles that I turned out better than she likely imagined.

Then again, Mrs. Frump, you really don't know what I do in my spare time... do you?

Darren Marlar
Voice Artist at DarrenMarlar.com

Introduction

My childhood was not at all normal. In fact, it was paranormal. I grew up with ghosts, poltergeist and with a strong fascination for the supernatural and occult. About 18-months ago, I set out to document some of my experiences in the book *My Haunted Life*. I was astounded by the interest in the stories and the topic in general, and soon started talking to family and friends about their own strange stories as I penned *My Haunted Life Too* and *My Haunted Life 3*[1]. What struck me during all of this is that actually, everyone has a strange story to tell. That is when I started the **My Haunted Life Too** website (http://www.myhauntedlifetoo.com) where people could submit their own strange tales. What I truly wasn't prepared for was the sheer diversity and in some instance, total bizarreness, of the stories that people submitted. The world is indeed a very strange place – or at least our perception of it is strange at times.

Of course, in reading other people's stories, I also recalled a few other incidents myself and included them on the site. So what follows is a set of strange and even downright scary tales

---

[1] All three books are ebooks but a compilation of them called *My Haunted Life Extreme Edition* is available in paperback as well.

submitted by visitors to the website along with a few more of my own. So settle back, relax and read and enjoy this collection of true scary stories submitted by people just like you. Oh – and do pop over and visit the site.

More Ghosts in the Machines...

My last book dealt with technology and the after life – how ghosts and in some instances perhaps demons, were more and more using technology to communicate with the living. I wasn't surprised then, to have a number of stories submitted that dealt with this very subject.

Voicemail

My Mother-in-Law passed away quite recently. She had been extremely ill with cancer and right before she died, they suspected that she had a second case of cancer too. She was still quite young at the age of 68 and lay comatose for the last few days of her life in the hospital. The morning that she died, my father-in-law was tending to her and trying to keep her as comfortable as possible. While he was there, her mobile phone rang but he ignored it, as he was busy. Three hours later, my mother-in-law passed away.

A few days later he checked the voicemail messages. What he heard on that voicemail really startled him, and later startled me. He only played me the message a few weeks ago. All that you hear is this strange breathing sound, blowing noises and static. It starts slowly but grows rapidly, then it gets slower again. The message lasts for about 2 minutes.

Was this a spirit telephone call? Whatever, it's rather creepy and I wouldn't want to hear it again.

Submitted by Bill.

A Voice From Beyond The Grave

When I was about six or seven years old I recall our home phone ringing. It was about 9pm at night and my Mum was busy in the other room so she asked me to answer it. I did so and at first I could only hear lots of static. I repeated over and over again,

"Hello? Hello?"

But no one answered. There was just all of that static. Thinking that it must have been a wrong number, I started to hang up. But then a voice caught me by surprise.

"Hello?" said the voice.

To my amazement, it sounded just like my grandfather. So I said,

"Grandpa? Grandpa? I can't hear you."

And he said something like, *"Hi, baby. How are you? Can I speak with your mommy?"*
I thought that it must be my mother's father, who is still alive, and so I gave my mom the phone and left the room. However, when she came out the room she had this weird look on her face. I asked her what was wrong and she said,

"That was your grandfather."

Well, of course I knew my own grandfathers' voice, but then she said,

"No, that was not my father, it was your dad's father."

I could not believe it even as a seven year old. How could it be my fathers' father as had died many, many years before when my dad was still just a little boy? My Mum said that he had called to see how we were doing and that he had finally got a chance to hear his first grand daughter's voice.

I was glad that I did answer the phone, because if my Mum had answered, I probably would not have had a chance to talk with him. My Mum said that after a few words, his voice just faded away back into the static.

Too bad there wasn't such thing as caller-ID back then. I have never had another paranormal experience-- one was enough.

Submitted by Anon.

Creepy Christmas Cell Phone

This story is about something very strange that happened at home during the Christmas break. My husband had placed his cell phone on our dining room table and turned it off for the evening. My purse was in our library, where my husband was playing a computer game with our daughter. In my purse was my cell phone, which was turned on. As my husband and daughter were playing, my cell phone rang. Of course, my husband picked it up and saw that it said that the incoming call was coming in from his cell phone!
He thought our son was playing a prank on him and ran into the room we were in and told him to stop messing around with his cell phone. We laughed at him and asked him what he was talking about. He said,

"Your phone just rang and it said the call was coming in from my phone!"

This is where things got even stranger. My son and I were both in the same room together talking and neither one of us had left that room. We weren't actually even in the same room as my husband's cell phone at all.

My husband checked his phone and sure enough, it was off just as he had left it. We still can't figure out how a call was registered on my phone from his when his phone was switched off and there was certainly no one in the room to make the call.

Strange indeed and we were all pretty mystified over the whole incident for sure!

Submitted by Anon.

Weird Call

Just over a week ago, I was lying in bed relaxing and trying to fall asleep. I had just turned off the TV and was about to turn over and try to get some sleep, but my cell phone, that I had already turned off and placed on charge, suddenly started vibrating. I decided to ignore it, but it turned on and then started ringing, I didn't recognize the number at all so I picked it up and said

"Hello,"

There was nothing but static on the other end of the phone and then the call was ended. I tried to call the number back, but was told that it was out of service.

Submitted by Anon.

The Dead Calling

My sister has had some pretty interesting activity on both her answering machine and her phones. I have heard one of the messages from the other side that was left on her answering machine. We know that someone or something, is trying to communicate with her using electronic energy as the mode. What we both want to know is how can we better receive these messages.

The messages are sometimes hard to make out, yet some of the words are very clear. These messages are very definitely not left by human vocal chords (that much we know). We do not know where to go for this. I mean, it is not like we can call the ghost busters or anything!

She recently has had a good friend pass away and I also have had a friend pass. It could be one of these two ladies, or it could be any lost soul in need of assistance.

Today's message said (as far as we could make out),

"I'm calling from the afterlife. Pick up the phone."
Submitted by Anon.

Finally, here is a twist on the Ghosts in The Machines theme. I would say that this was an example of a ghost communicating over radio... but it's even stranger than that.

Patient Speaks on the Radio While in Surgery

I was listening to a call-in talk show on the radio while driving in Los Angeles. The announcer came back from an advertising break to speak with his next caller and to my great surprise it turned out to be my great aunt calling in. She would not give the announcer her name, but she said,

"For those in your listening audience who know me, they will recognize me by this song"

She then began to sing an old tune that she used to sing to me when I was a child. I thought I was asleep at the wheel! She went on to say that she was in the hospital having an operation.

"I haven't told many people, not even my family, but they were doing this surgery because they thought I had cancer. They have just found out I don't!"

The next day, I called my mother to tell her what I had heard on the radio. She quizzed me at length about the actual time of day that I had heard my great aunt say she did not have cancer. It turned out that my mother had been at the hospital with my aunt and was there at precisely the time that I had heard her sing and then talk on the radio. The problem was that, at that time, she was still in surgery! In fact, at the time of the 'broadcast' the doctors had not even yet left the operating room to tell my mother that my aunt did not have cancer.

Ever since that experience I have believed in the paranormal and the great beyond.

Submitted by Anon.

The Intervening Daemon

In *My Haunted Life,* I related a story of how when driving on a dirt forest road in Canada as a student, I had got a little carried away. Tearing down the gravel track was fun. At some point however, a voice from behind me yelled "*Slow down.*" Had I not followed that voices instruction, I would almost certainly have been maimed or died, as the road suddenly took a hairpin curve around that was hidden by the trees on either side. I pulled over shaking in disbelief and peered into the steep ravine over which I almost veered. The voice saved my skin that day whatever that voice was.

Years later, I read a book by Anthony Peake called *The Daemon: A Guide To Your Extraordinary Secret Self.* In the book Anthony discusses at length, the proposition that all consciously aware beings consist of not one, but two separate consciousness's - everyday consciousness and that of the Daemon, a higher being that seems to possess knowledge of future events. I suddenly understood that the voice I had heard from the back seat was indeed that of my own Daemon.

The reaction to my story in certain quarters was one of disbelief. The very idea that a disincarnate voice would shout and scream at me to slow down and in doing so, save my life, was just too strange for them. However, I know that I am not the only person to have such an experience.....

The Voice in the Wilderness

This happened to me about ten years ago. My wife and I were heading out with some friends camping. My wife was cooking some dinner on the stove and we were about to settle down for the evening. I decided to go for a run and said that I would get back before she had finished making dinner.

As I started to jog down a narrow trail, I entered a woody area of the track and I could see that there was a sharp drop ahead of me. I thought it would be a slope that I could run down, but my head exploded with voices telling me to stop. I heard another voice behind me that yelled,

"STOP BRUCE!"

I stopped and walked to the beginning of the slope only to find to my horror that part of the slope was missing and had been replaced by a huge hole. A sinkhole. Had I kept going I would have fallen about 20 feet down into this hole and would have killed myself. My wife wouldn't have had any idea where I was and I didn't have a cell phone on me.

What scares me more is that I could have spent a long, long time down there starving to death. Thank God for the voices in my head!

Submitted by Anon.

My Driving Angel

Driving home from my boss's dinner party at midnight, I had an experience that I'd like to share with you. I hadn't drunk too much that night and I was taking the drive home slow. However, at some point on the way home I dozed off; actually fell asleep at the wheel. Suddenly my head was raised from the lowered position it was in and my eyes were forced open. I saw a metal guardrail coming right at me. I was suddenly driving at 85 miles per hour. As fast as my eyes were opened, something grabbed my wrists and moved the steering wheel. The car glanced past the guardrail. I could hear the screeching tires and I thought for a second that the car was going to tip over. It didn't.

My guardian angel saved my life that night. I am sure of it. I have never attended a party since.

Submitted by Anon.

Protective Presences

Not all ghostly experiences are frightening or even negative. In fact, some are reassuring and supportive, as if a family member, or an angelic being is looking after your interests. I have had several stories of this nature submitted to the site and they make interesting reading.

The Vigil

My father's death was imminent. About 24 hours before he passed, I went to sit outside on a tree stump in a corner of the yard. My father's home was in a heavily wooded, sparsely populated residential area. As I sat there amongst the trees, feeling the breeze, listening to the birdsong, enjoying the quiet of nature, I began to notice a stream of figures slowly fill the driveway and the path up to the house. These figures were unidentifiable as any specific individual. It seemed as though their facial features were blurred, even faceless. Some wore long white robes with hoods drawn up over their heads. Others were in regular clothing. There were both male and female figures. It was a very somber procession, and eventually, about 200 were there, silently standing in place.

They did not move; they did not interact with one

another; they did not speak to me. They simply stood quietly, packed closely together, waiting. In the ensuing 24 hours, more figures began appearing within the house at the far end of the house from my father's bedroom at first, then slowly filtering in to the living room, down the hallway, and finally, a few hours before his death, they filled his room completely.

Again, they were silent and non-interactive with each other, although I began to feel warm acknowledgement from some of them. I still could not discern facial features, but I felt immense comfort coming directly from them. They surrounded my father, patiently standing there. I got the sense they could have stood there for years; there was no sense of time associated with them at all. The peace and calm energy that filled that space during their presence was overwhelming.

Eventually, my father took his last breath. A minute or two later, the figures began fading, one by one, beginning with the ones nearest to him and then farther away, in the reverse order in which they had appeared. A small group of about 40 remained outside, lining the path to the front door and down the driveway. When the funeral director came a few hours later, as my father's body was driven away, they slowly faded as well.

I will never forget the serenity of that time, in what might otherwise be such upheaval and grief. I truly have no doubt that my father was in no way alone in his transition, and that there is certainly another type of existence after this one.

Submitted by Lori.

Ghostly Angel?

I usually wake up in the middle of the night. It seems to be a habit that I have developed. Anyway, this one night I woke up and I saw something standing at the bottom of my bed. A bright white light shone around the figure and I couldn't make anything else out. It was such a soothing experience, not scary at all. That's my only paranormal experience.

Submitted by Al.

The Old Man in the Graveyard

I was at the crematorium just after my boyfriend died. I was putting flowers' on his plot. As you might imagine, I was very upset. I just missed him so much. However, I also think that sometimes our emotions can play tricks on us, so I am not sure if I imagined this or if it really actually happened.

I was there kneeling by the plot crying and talking to him, telling him how much I missed him when all of a sudden, I looked round and there behind me was an old man. I still do not know where he appeared from as it was early morning and the crematorium was completely empty when I arrived.

The "Old Man" smiled at me and said,

"Do not worry and be upset. He is okay and you will in time learn to deal with the loss of your loved one. He knows you loved him very much. It will get easier."

I looked at him, smiled and said thank you. I looked back at the plot and then behind me to look at the old man... and he was gone.

At the time, I was too upset to think anything of it and simply thought he must have gone through the entrance. But when I left, I began to wonder where the old man had gone, as the entrance was quite a walk from where I was and he would still have been in my sight when I looked up. I wonder if I had been crying for longer and didn't see him walk out the gate? But, still today, I think about it. Can a ghost come to us and look human? Maybe he was a spirit helping me come to terms with my grief. Or, was I such an emotional wreck, that I did not even notice him leave?

Submitted by Anon.

Near Death Experience

When I was nine years old, I was a very sick child as a result of suffering from various illnesses. I was constantly in and out of hospitals. At one point, I had been sick for a long time and, by all accounts, I was close to death. All I can remember is seeing what looked like a man surrounded by light. No facial features, no distinctive marks, just the figure of a man bathed in life. He asked me directly if I was ready to go. I didn't want to go and wanted to live. He explained that he would never hurt me, but I kept wondering what would happen to my parents. It was then that I felt completely filled with love and energy. The figure was gone but that feeling remained with me for a long time afterwards. With my health in the state it was in, I should have suffered more than I did. I didn't die and I'm alive today to take care of my parents.

Every now and then I still feel the energy of that being taking care of me, healing me from within.

Submitted by Anon.

Ghost Writer

I had an experience in Gloucester Place, London a few years ago. In the night, I was taken very ill and I was 'visited' by a beautiful, sophisticated young Victorian woman who had been an author during her life. Naturally I was terrified, firstly by the appearance of a ghost and secondly, by the fact she had come to help me over to the other side. She regarded me as a kindred spirit and persuaded me that death and the next life were nothing to be afraid of. If I wanted to let go, then all I had to do was to take her hand, and she would guide me through to the next world. After what felt like a couple of hours in the company of this charming, sweet character, my fever lifted and slowly she began to vanish with the onset of morning. I'm extremely grateful to her for helping me in my struggle to survive and I am sure we will meet again - hopefully, in many, many years' time!

Submitted by Graham.

My Protective Grandmother

As a child, my mother was very concerned about me, as I would talk to people in my sleep. I later began sleepwalking all the time. Although she was concerned about the talking in my sleep and my sleepwalking, she always played along and acted as though she wanted to meet my invisible friend. During the middle of one night, I woke up to see, what looked like an old woman sitting at the end of my bed. It was a dark, shadowy figure, but I could tell from the hairstyle that it was female. I literally hid under my duvet and I never told anyone else about it.

After that my sleepwalking and talking ended and I forgot about the whole thing. A few years later, after my mother died, I was going through her stuff and found a picture of her mother. I instantly knew that this was the lady who was sitting at the end of my bed. The hairstyle gave it away.

A few years after that a friend dragged me to a spiritualist meeting and that same grandmother came through. She apologized for scaring me as a child and admitted that she often came to visit me. She also told me that my Uncle James spent a lot of time around me. I was freaked out on one hand, but isn't it comforting to know that we aren't always alone?

Submitted by Anon.

Grandma's Ghost and the Babysitter

My Grandma passed over back in 1967. It was a shock to all that knew her for she was only 57 years old. She was a firebrand and left behind her loving husband, three daughters and three sons. Naturally, the loss of your mother at such a young age was hard for all of her children. They all missed her spark and often spoke about her.

A year, or so, had passed and the family was beginning to recover after the wake of such and unexpected death. Grandma's oldest daughter S, who looked just like Grandma, had my brother and I to take care of, which kept her busy. Mom went out with her friends one night and had hired a local sitter to watch my brother and I. As the night went on the kids went to bed and the sitter had asked her boyfriend to come over. The next thing I knew there was a scream downstairs as someone walked in on the couple, who I presume were up to the usual teenage activities. The sitter started to apologize to the person she thought was our mother. An argument took place, which I thought was strange, as my mother was not confrontational. I remember the intruder saying,

"Get your clothes on and go home, you whore."

The sitter left in disarray, she wasn't paid and I went back to sleep. I thought mom had come home early.

The next morning I came downstairs with my brother to find my mother on the phone. She was talking to the sitter and asking,

"Why did you leave my kids all alone last night?"

The sitter apparently said that she had been sent home. I'm not sure if she repeated why she was sent home. My mother looked amazed and said *"I certainly did not send you home."*

My mother later told me that the sitter had said that someone came in the house and told the sitter to leave, and it certainly looked like Mum. I later told my mother that I had actually heard what was going on, and asked what had upset her. She told me that she hadn't come home early that night. She had been out with her boyfriend, at a club dancing. So, I presume Grandma came in and confronted the horny babysitter.

Go figure?

Submitted by Anon.
Uncle's Last Visit
It was 1984 and I was about 6 years old at that time. It was the first time that I realized that I had this third eye. In my younger years, I saw a lot of creepy things, but this one I could say was my very first experience!

My uncle Al had just died in a car crash a few days ago. We were so very close. He used to play with me and even made a swing for us to use for an afternoon nap. One night, a day after his funeral, I had some very strange feelings and I had this urge to keep my eyes open despite being very sleepy. For three hours, I just stared at the ceiling and the window. Then I prayed to God...

"Lord, help me to fall asleep," because I was so tired.

Suddenly, when I looked up to the Sacred Heart of Jesus image that was on our wall I saw the face of my uncle who had just departed, happily looking at me. I felt scared, but relaxed and then I closed my eyes and fell asleep.

Submitted by Marilou

Haunted Pictures

Another area of paranormal activity that I apparently have in common with some our readers, is having experienced paintings and pictures that seemed to be haunted. I collected several haunted picture stories from friends and relatives for my books including the one I liked best from my Dad. He recalled asking his parents if they were going to take a picture of a man that was at the top of the stairs in their temporary apartment when they moved home only to be looked at strangely and told it was an empty picture frame......

The Elvis Presley Poster

I come from Serbia, but I am now living in Sweden. All my life, I have been a huge fan of Elvis Presley, so I had a big Elvis poster on my door. It had been there for about two years and one evening, the poster fell down on the floor. I hung it up again, but it fell down again. I cleaned the door and hung it up again and it still fell down. I did the same thing about 10 times. Finally, I gave up, threw it in the basket and went to bed. The first thing I heard on the radio the next morning was that Elvis had died in his home - the same evening when my poster fell to the floor.

Submitted by Tim

A Possessed Painting?

I have started reading all of the stories on this blog as I have always had an interest in the paranormal and thought that I would share my own creepy experience with you.

At home we have a main floor family room, which looks up to a deck that looks down into the family room. We were getting ready for supper one night. My son was upstairs in his bedroom reading with his Aunt. My wife, mother, daughter and myself were all in the kitchen below. The kitchen is open concept to the family room, so you can see pretty well everything in the family room. I was standing at the edge of both rooms. All of a sudden, I heard a noise coming from the deck. I went to investigate and saw that a large framed picture of a tiger, on the wall above the deck, was the source of the noise. I actually saw the picture moving then, *something* picked it up and hurled that picture, which is actually quite heavy, into the family room. It made a loud thud when it hit the floor and everybody came running to see what had caused all that noise.

Nobody believed me when I told then what I saw. I think it's important to mention that my father had passed away suddenly a few years ago. I put this picture temporarily on the wall again and tried holding it there, but it still moved several millimeters.

That picture flying off the wall was the creepiest thing I have ever witnessed, even though after my fathers death, we have heard many strange noises in our home.

Submitted by Anon.

Ouija Board Troubles

After an experience with an Ouija board, I recommend people stay away from them. They are unsafe and attract unwanted things...

Ouija Board Ghost

My mother's friend's family lived in a house that was located in one of the oldest recorded towns in Texas. The friend's Mother, who lived there, had seen the ghost of a Civil War soldier appear there several times. He would just appear and stare at her and then disappear again.

My mom and her friend played with a Ouija board in that house and my mom said that the furniture in the room started shaking loudly and also the drawers in a piece of furniture started moving in and out.

Submitted by Anon.

Never Abuse The Undead

My cousin and I were doing a sleepover one time when we were teenagers. We had an Ouija board and I wanted to try it out. He didn't. He went to bed, but I stayed up and decided to try it out. I put it on a table and asked it the usual questions. It didn't work, so getting bored I started to ask stupid questions. I asked if the spirits were too dumb to understand me. Nothing happened. A few days later I had forgotten about it.

Over the following weekend I had been asleep and woke up in a sweat. I sat up in my bed and saw what looked like a man, kneeling on the floor. He had black hair, a long beard and he looked up at me. He said

"My name is John and I am not f* * * *g stupid,"

I was terrified. He stood up and started screaming at me. I couldn't hear the words, but the room got deathly cold very quickly. I managed to find the strength to jump out of bed and ran into the other room from where I could hear him ranting for about thirty or so minutes. Then everything else is a blank.

I woke up in bed the next morning and I have never been near an Ouija board since then.

Submitted by James

Haunted Houses

I grew up in a house that I thought was haunted. In fact, I hardly dare sleep there and after I was 18, I would get drunk in order to sleep there, it was that bad. So I do sympathize with the readers who shared these experiences.

A Haunted House

We moved into our house on Halloween in the year 2002. It's located in "downeast" Maine about a mile and a half from the seashore and it was built in the 1880s and at one time, it was a pretty famous for chicken canning. One of the sons of the former owners was killed in action in WWII. We still have the love letters that he wrote to his 3-month bride before he was killed right before the end of the war, in 1945.

The older gentleman, who lived in the house prior to the people we bought it from, had actually died in the house and it was a few days before anyone found him. But, it appears that a young girl is haunting the place and we don't know who she is or why. I have seen her and so has my father.

The property also seems to be haunted because as you walk by the windows we often see someone out in the fields around the house, walking towards the old goat pens, only to disappear. The person in the field is wearing a white shirt and black suspenders.

Here are some of the weird things I've encountered.

We were doing renovations, having the roof replaced and having a dormer put in the upstairs bathroom. One day, when the workers were not there, my father and I were the only people in the house. I was upstairs in my bedroom and my Dad was downstairs in the library, directly below my room. (There is a staircase that runs down the wall outside my door). He was sitting in his chair opposite the door and saw a girl come down the stairs, turn away from him, and go into the dining room. He thought it was me so he called out to me, but I was upstairs and hadn't moved. About 20 minutes later, it happened again. We got up and searched, but no one was around except us. The night that I saw her, I was laying in bed looking out the window when I felt someone standing over me. I looked to the side without moving and saw her face hovering over my bed. It was oval shaped and in sharp contrast, all whites and blacks. All I could see was her face. She was looking down at me with no expression and then, she wasn't there anymore. I wasn't afraid, I'm surprised to say, I just felt like she was looking in on me.

On Christmas Eve one year, I walked into the dining room to find 2 dead earthworms on the dining room floor. I have no idea where they came from. Needless to say in December, in Maine, the ground outside is frozen. There was no dirt on them either; they were just laid out like a gift. We have a full basement as well, so there is no way they came up out of the ground and through the floor boards. I called my folks in to see and it was a curious moment, but we threw them away and went on with whatever. An hour later, I came back through and there were two more worms laid out in the exact same spot! We checked and the other two were still in the trash. Nothing more after that, but it was still weird.

While we're working away, my older sister who lives next door watches the property for us. There is a small figurine of Uncle Sam that came from a Red Rose tea box that sits on the kitchen windowsill. Several times my sister has come over after no one has been there for weeks to find that figurine moved to the kitchen table more than 5 feet away, or to the kitchen counter, which is even farther.

My nieces were cleaning the house for us, knocking down cobwebs and generally keeping the dust down, but refused to do so after they heard someone crying upstairs in the empty house.

You will hear footsteps in parts of the house where people are not about, you will hear and feel doors open and close, changes in the air pressure is readily apparent, only to check and find that nothing had moved. Drawers in a certain bureau containing board games will open regularly. You can hear it opening and then go look and the drawers are all opened; pulled all the way out.

At night there is always a feeling of being followed around the downstairs of the house, but never on the second floor. And, there are certain rooms in the house that always feel occupied, or you feel that someone is outside staring through the curtains at you, even if the window is closed and the curtains pulled shut.

Then there is the Victorian Gentleman that I saw. It was late at night, around 1 a.m. My sister and I were cleaning the house from top to bottom in preparation for my parents coming home for the holidays. I was standing in the kitchen facing my sister who was in the dining room doorway. We were chatting about what had been done versus what needed to be done, when behind her, I saw the upper shoulder and lapel of a man's suit walk into the jelly cupboard; a converted door that once lead to the basement. I can imagine the look of shock on my face because my sister immediately asked what was behind her. I told her, and we checked, but of course there was no one there, and there wouldn't be, it's a solid wood door that leads to into a six-inch deep pantry. He was all gray and tall. All I could see was the shoulder of a suit jacket and a lapel, but the cut reminded me very much of a frock coat.

Submitted by Anon.

The Ghost Who Locked Me Out of My House

About 17 years ago, I was living in Montana in a house that was pretty far outside of the city limits. Right from the very start, the house did strange things. The lights would cut out, as would the T.V., which would also start changing channels on its own. Items would move from place to place.

One night I went outside to feed my dog and I noticed my dog was staring at the back door of the house and making noises. I thought that was strange, so I looked around and saw a woman dressed in very old clothing, likely from the Wild West era, standing by the door. When she saw me looking at her, she closed the door and disappeared into thin air. I was pretty shaken up by it and ran over to the door. It was locked. I ran around to the front of the house and found my two sons and my wife sitting in the T.V room watching T.V. I honestly thought they were pulling a prank on me. They denied it, so I just tried to forget about it and went back outside to feed the dog.

I kept the door open, and placed a brick there to keep it open. I went over to the dog and got back to my chore of feeding the dog. He started whining again, so I looked back around and there was that lady again. This time the door closed onto the brick and she disappeared. I was beside myself. I ran back around and accused my family of playing pranks on me. They assured me they wouldn't do such a thing and slowly I started to believe them.

After doing some research I found out that a lady had lived in that house all alone and that she was murdered one night. She had been buried somewhere on the property. We still have happenings every now and again and she still creeps me out, but I hope she is resting in peace.

Submitted by Anon.

The Old Man

The strangest thing that happened to me was when I was growing up in Tennessee. My mother was ill and out of work and we lived in a very old house near Knoxville. We all slept in the same bedroom, my mother, my younger sister and I. This arrangement was needed in order to close off the other rooms for better heating.

My story takes place late one night. We had gone to bed early and I had been sleeping soundly until I suddenly woke up for no reason and had a feeling that someone was watching me. I turned over to look toward my mother, who was asleep in the bed with my younger sister. I then noticed something that really terrified me. Sitting in an old chair, between the two beds, was an elderly looking gentleman. He looked real with graying hair, and he was wearing a white long-sleeve shirt with dark slacks. He was just sitting there staring right at me. I forced myself to turn away and tried to think of a reason for what I had just seen. I couldn't find one and couldn't find enough courage to turn over and look again. I just closed my eyes and tried to go back to sleep. I didn't tell anyone about this sighting.

A few years later, I was at a family gathering for a meal. After our meal, we were making small talk when my younger sister brought up our childhood and the earlier years at that old house. To my surprise, she mentioned that the only thing that really bothered her was the old man who she had seen in our bedroom where our mother slept with us.

Submitted by Anon.

Mr. Skeleton

It was 1960 and we had just built our dream home in Texas. It was good land and the area around our house was all streams, rustic countryside; and the land our house was built on had no record of having had any structure built on it before. The owner had told us that he had used the land for grazing cattle.

My wife had two huge experiences in that house. I was out working and my wife was busy at home working on one of her hobbies. She noticed that the bedroom door was open and decided to go down and close it. As she neared the door, she saw the strange shape of a woman in a white dress drifting out of the room and into the wall opposite. She put that first experience down to having had too many glasses of wine with her dinner. Later, she was folding laundry in the bedroom, when she saw a black apparition that took the form of a skeleton walking past the bedroom door. It headed towards my office and vanished. The next day, she was lying on the bed when the skeletal form returned and walked into the bedroom. She sat upright in fear and it turned to stare at her. Then it disappeared. That night she told me what happened but I didn't really pay much attention. This was our dream home after all.

A few months later, she was staying with her sister and I was in my office working on a drawing when I looked up and saw this black form in the doorway. It solidified and I saw that it was the skeletal form she had spoken about. In disbelief I reached into my draw to find the gun I kept in there, but by the time I had fished it out, the form had disappeared. We sold the house as quickly as we could and moved away. That was the strangest experience I ever had and I have no intention of ever repeating it.

Submitted by Anon.

Lady in Black

When I was still in elementary school, around 1995, our classes only lasted half a day so I would go home and stay there alone until my parents returned from work, which wasn't usually until about six in the evening. Each afternoon, as I watched television alone in the living room, I would notice the silhouette of a Black Lady going up the stairs. I only saw her out of the side of my eye and when I look at her directly, she disappeared. At first, I thought this was just my imagination, or probably something wrong with my eyesight.

One day, as my older brother and I were playing and telling stories, he mentioned that sometimes he noticed a Black Lady-like shadow going up the stairs and eventually vanishing. That's when I realized that what I had been seeing was not simply my imagination. Since that point, whenever I was alone at home, I would go hang outside or ask my friends to play in our house until my parents came back.
As I grew older, the Black Lady's appearances became less and less. Or, maybe it just came out of my mind. The Black Lady is not appearing anymore, but I can't say I miss her...

Boy in the Sailor Suit
About 30 years ago, a friend of a friend's sister was getting married, and I somehow found myself invited to the stag. I'd never been to the

house before, and as we waited for the groom to arrive, the bride's mother insisted that we have a cup of tea. We sat chatting about nothing in particular when, out of the corner of my eye, I became aware of a young boy, perhaps 7 or 8, dressed in a sailor suit go into the kitchen, and thought nothing of it.

As we sat, the boy came out of the kitchen, and stood, very politely, beside my chair. I turned and said,

"Hello, what is your name?"

He very politely introduced himself as James, then chattered away for a couple of minutes about school, games and the cat, before announcing that he was going upstairs. Half an hour later, as we were leaving, I shouted up the stairs,

"Bye-bye, James."

Our host looked startled, and asked who James was? It turned out there were no children in the house, let alone one wearing a sailor suit. I never went back...
Submitted by Alan.

The Cigar Smoking Ghost

I bought a 4-storey stone house and farm almost 11 years ago. It is 4,800 square feet, high ceilings, and six fireplaces and was built in 1805 and on the National Registry of Historic Places in south central PA. I'm a carpenter and I specialize in historic renovations having moved there from the DC area. When I went to closing, I told the couple that I was buying it from that I would be disappointed if there was no ghost. She laughed and said the ghost smokes pipes and cigars and makes a lot of racket, but is harmless. I had lived in a very haunted house in Minneapolis when I was young and I like ghosts!

About a week after moving in, we got hit with an ice storm so I was lying in bed reading when around 10am I suddenly smell very strongly cigar smoke. This is a farm with other houses a block or more away and it's January so the windows are closed. I got up and said out loud

"I know this is your house but it's mine too and I don't smoke and would you please smoke out side."

After that, you could smell his pipes and cigars on one of the three covered porches.

About every three months, he would smoke in the house again and would have to be reminded, although lately he been more obedient. He walks around a lot and I've stopped walking around with a gun when I hear him as I train border collies to herd sheep and no one could walk up anywhere near here with out them raising hell. Submitted by Mark

A Haunted Barroom

My children, roommate and I lived in a home that was the first barroom in Somerset, MA, down by the old colony area. I would literally hear furniture moving around upstairs where there wasn't any furniture. There was always a strong smell of alcohol in the dirt cellar, where I would hear voices of many and noises-like china being stacked. My roommate and I witnessed a toy in the children's room that went off multiple times even after I removed the batteries. Lights in the house would turn on in the middle of the night.

The telephone was actually off of its receiver one night but it woke me up from the loud busy signal coming from it-no one was in the house other than me. It would also sound like my plants, which were hanging in certain windows, would come crashing to floor, but when I looked, no plants were on the floor. There was also constant loud creaking of the old barn board floorboards, like people were walking around.

Window Watcher

I had one strange experience once that I would like to share with you. I don't particularly believe in paranormal stuff, but this was a strange story.

My parents were gone to a wedding and my sister was out with her boyfriend. Having the house to myself, I decided I would shower and then watch some TV in my room. My room is situated on the highest floor of the house and to get to my bathroom, I had to walk down the stairs to my room, open my door and turn left to arrive at the bathroom door. At the time, my bathroom door had been left open.

I got my clothes from my room and I walked downstairs, but out of the corner of my eye I saw something just outside the window on the far wall of the bathroom. I thought it was a dove at first. But, as I turned my head to look directly at it, I saw that it was blurry and then I noticed that it wasn't a bird at all. It looked like a face. With two barely recognizable eyeholes, a faded black hole where the mouth would be, and what looked to be a depression for a nose.

As I stared at this, it didn't move, but it did seem to be fading away. I was pretty freaked out by this time so, after what seemed to be a minute of just staring at it, trying to find a reasonable explanation for what it was, I reached my hand into the bathroom and flicked the light switch off. I could still see it but it was not as noticeable because of the light glare on the bathroom window. I was so freaked out by this strange occurrence and I didn't want to go near it. I backed up into my room, turned on the bedroom light, and sat in my bed trying to make sense of it. I didn't go back downstairs again until my parents returned home the next day.

Invisible Ghost

At home in Michigan, I had just gone to bed and I was lying around with my dog when he started to completely go crazy! I looked around the room for something that could be bothering him when suddenly I felt my arm being pulled down against the bed. I looked to see what was constricting me and I saw nothing. Then I heard heavy breathing and I feel something close to me. I could actually feel the pressure on my arm getting stronger and stronger until it stopped.

Later that night I saw a depression in the mattress that looked like someone was standing on my bed, but there was nobody there. I didn't know what to do and had never had an experience like this before. Nothing has happened since so I have no idea what to make of that incident.

Unseen Presence in My Bedroom

When I was a child, my parents lived in Ontario, Canada. I had just gone to bed one night and was watching TV with my cat. My cat suddenly got scared and freaked out. I looked around the room and all of a sudden something grabbed my ankles and pulled me down the bed. I remember being pulled very angrily down to the bottom of the bed, but I couldn't see anything. Then it was like something was sitting on the bottom of the bed next to me. I could see the depression in the mattress. I got up, left the room and would never sleep in that bedroom again.

What Are You Going to Do? Shoot A Ghost?

In about 1976, I moved from the Chicago area to Minneapolis to live with a girl friend. I'm originally from Topeka Kansas and now live out east.

Anyway, we were renting a Victorian house with another girl from our high school and a couple; he being older and a spy working for the army. This

Victorian house was on Lyndale Ave. I'm not sure now of the spelling, but it was totally haunted! The ghosts, as we were sure there was more than one, were very active.

My then girl friend would see this old man standing behind her in the many built-ins with mirrors and, when turning around, would see nothing and upon looking back in the mirror, he would be right there again. This ghost would stomp around at night, open, doors and windows - even in the winter, and always an hour or two after we were all asleep.

One night I got up to use the bathroom and as I was headed back to our bedroom, (we always left the bathroom light on); someone was standing in front our door! It was an old man, short with a beard and I thought at first it was Walt, the Army spy and sometime boy friend of this hot farm girl from Illinois we were going to school with.

Anyway I walked to within a few steps of this old man asking "Walt? Walt?" Well, then I realized it was an old man; older than Walt, who was much older than us anyway. I stood there petrified for what might had been two minutes, but seemed much longer. I could see him perfectly, but right through him as well! At some point I lunged and he disappeared. I ran into my girl friends room and grabbed a WW 11 P 38 I'm sure I was too young at the time to own. After hearing my over exited story she was like "what are you going to do, shoot a ghost?"

Submitted by Mark

Crying Lady

This happened when I was about 16 years old. My dad had just scolded me for coming home late. I went outside and sat by our pool to cry my heart out. When I looked at the swing there was an old lady sitting there looking at me. Immediately, I knew she was an apparition because she was almost transparent. I couldn't move, I thought I was yelling for help, but nothing seemed to come out. I closed my eyes and when I opened them again, she was gone.

I saw her again as I was on my way out with some friends. She was motioning for me not to go. I thought I was imagining this and went out just the same. We got into a head on collision accident. I was sitting in the front seat without a seat belt on, but I was the only one not hurt. What I felt was like arms that pinned me to the seat.

The last time I saw her was right after I had

taken a bath. I decided to say something to her.
"*What do you want? I don't know who you are and you are scaring me, get out I do not want to see you again.*"

After going to bed that night I was woken by a crying sound. It seemed to come from a lady. I figured that it was she and so I said,

"*I am sorry for getting angry earlier, but I was scared.*"

From that time on I never heard or saw her again. EVER!

Submitted by Luisa

Albert

My family owns a hunting camp up near Atlanta and we go there each year for a week or so. One year, my father invited a few of his friends and their families to the place. The house that we owned was built in the 1800's and my father had rebuilt it from a ruin. The previous owners name was inscribed at the back of the house on a large stone near the foundation. His name was Albert.

Each year, weird things would happen in the house; items would go missing, strange noises, a weird sound that sounded like gunfire, all kinds of things. That year we put some of my dad's friends and their families up on folding lawn chairs in the den. A few nights into the trip, several of the guests complained about a deep, loud scream coming from the living room. One of the guests turned the light on and to his horror, found his wife being 'eaten up' by her own chair. The chair was actually bending her body and wrapping around it. It took three grown men to get the chair off her and that family left the following morning.

My father always said it was Albert and that his ghost took a dislike to the man. His wife was disliked in my fathers friends circle and maybe the ghost took a dislike to her too?
Submitted by Anon.

Old Woman
About ten years ago, I was staying with one of my friends and her family in Memphis. They lived in an old house and I have always gotten the creeps when I was there alone. One evening I went to a movie with my friend and we came back late. We walked into the kitchen and to our amazement, we saw an old woman standing against the door. She was almost bent double and up against the door as though she were listening. She turned,

looked at us and smiled. I walked towards her and she disappeared.

It was freaky but that spirit didn't seem to mean us any harm.

Submitted by Anon.

The Victorian House Basement

My girl friend was going to night school and I was drinking beer and watching TV one night, when Patty, a roommate, knocked on my door and wanted to know if my girlfriend was around. I told her that she would not be home until midnight and she complained about the spookiness of the house and wanted me to sit in her room with her and watch TV there while she did her study work, as her boyfriend was out of town. So I'm sitting there watching TV and drinking a beer while she studies and we hear some one enter the front door. This was about 9pm and she asked,

"Is that Kathy?"

I was sure that Kathy wasn't due home for hours and Patty told me that her boyfriend was out of town for the week so we both got up and looked down the stairs where we saw the shadowy figure of a man walk from the vestibule into the kitchen. We looked at each other and although scared, decided to investigate. The house had more than one ghost; the worst being a crying baby, but this was a first. We went down to the kitchen together and the door to the basement was open, and we never left that open! This old Victorian house had a basement you would not want to go down in daylight let alone at night! Patty was a farm girl and said,

"You've got a shotgun don't you?"

"Of course," I said, and we went back up and armed ourselves.

She walked in front of me with a 20-gauge pump and I was behind her with a pistol. We went down the stairs and saw that someone or something had turned the light on (just a bulb hanging from a socket so you had to go down and pull a string). As we reached the last step, Patty with shotgun in hand asked if I wanted to keep going? I said *"No way,"* and we walked backwards up the stairs, closed the door and none of us ever went down there again that I can recall!

Submitted by Mark

A Ghostly Dog - A Scary Ghost Story

When we first moved into our house in Houston, Texas, we had a few strange experiences. The house wasn't old - perhaps 10-years old, by the time we moved in, so we really couldn't explain the occurrences. The first thing we noticed was what appeared to be a dog walking by just outside the Den windows in the back yard. It was a big dog and moving slowly. The first few times, we just assumed it belonged to a neighbor but once we go to know them, we learned no one locally had a big dog. Occasionally, I would run out across the kitchen and out the back door, but there was never any dog to be found. After a while, we just got used to the ghostly dog in the yard. After all, he didn't bark or bite!

The next thing was crying. We would hear crying coming from an upstairs room, but whenever we went up the stairs, we found no one there and no reason for the sound. Eventually, the crying sounds stopped. Who knows whom the dog belonged to or why it would pass by the back window so often? As for the crying, we did find the previous owners had lost a small child......

Submitted by G. Michael Vasey

The Haunted House in Detroit

I live in Detroit. My family has lived there for many years. Whenever we passed a small wooden house in Highland Park, my dad always pointed it out as a very haunted house that his grandfather built. My grandfather ran his business from the house and my father always told me this story. Apparently, there was a dark little room in the back with a painting of an old fashioned hearse on the wall and a small table. Every so often, the building got cold and some very strange things would happen. Apparently my grandfather would hear a loud shaking noise at night, and in the morning the small table would be in a different location. If you were in the room you could hear the sounds of horses galloping.

My grandfather got sick of moving this table back to its original position and decided to put it outside. The next morning it had moved back to its original position. It was said that the original owners of the table had been practicing Ouija on the table. My grandfather was a hard man and he decided to burn it rather than put up with its antics.

The building my grandfather built was demolished a few years ago and the developers are now talking about building a house on the land. There are two reasons not to buy the house they build, firstly, crime in Highland Park is dangerous and secondly, that land is probably still haunted!

Submitted by Anon.

House Occupied....

We moved into a new house around ten years ago. From the first day, I thought it was haunted. I have heard, seen and felt things that you can't explain away. My husband thought I was going insane until the day he was up late watching a football game. He turned his head and a big, old black man was looking straight at him. He now believes me.

One night, I woke up in the middle of the night and I instantly felt as though I were not alone. I could feel it in the air. I couldn't fall back to sleep, so I decided to watch some TV. Even though I was wide-awake, I could not get out of bed. It was as though my body was still asleep, but my eyes were open. Eventually, I managed to get out of bed and I went downstairs. It was insanely quiet. No clocks ticking, no creaking. Nothing. All of a sudden, I saw the man that I presume my husband had also seen previously walk through the door. I could see him vividly. He was carrying a lit torch. As soon as he left, I could hear the clock ticking and the sound of the wind blowing outside. It was freaky.

My dog spends a lot of time staring at the walls. My sister saw a man (a different man) looking back at her from a mirror. My mother won't stay at the house since a man screaming at her to get the hell up waked her up.

My niece was taking care of painting a room in the house while we were on vacation. She said that she was told by an elderly black man to leave the house, and that she wasn't welcome. She called me later that day to ask me who was in the house and we had no idea. Nobody was in the house.

My father said that one time he actually asked if there were spirits there and of so, to give him a sign. A door slammed shut and he was told to leave. That's proof enough for me. My father is a big six-foot ex-miner. He will not visit us anymore. Has anyone else had experiences like this?
Submitted by Anon.

Haunted Locations

Of course, many stories defy classification. They are really about creepy locations in which events simply seem to happen leaving a lasting impression on those affected.

Something Dangerous in the Woods?

In May of 2000, my friends and I were out walking on an early evening. My friend, Dave, wanted to go to the cemetery just for fun; we wanted to get spooked, I guess. So we agreed. We went through all the graves and I found it creepy and felt as if someone was watching me from far away. So I looked behind me thought I saw someone hiding behind a tree, but perhaps my mind was playing tricks on me?

My friends were gathered around a tombstone; they found it interesting, because it had some markings on it. My friend and I went on to wander around when all of a sudden we heard someone crying out in the woods. We decided to go out and see what was going on. We were half way into the woods when my friend saw something behind a bush. She was scared to go see what it was. So I went first and as I was walking, I saw two green eyes looking right at me! I just started screaming and I grabbed my friend, who was petrified, and we ran all the way back to the car.

My other friends were still out in the cemetery and we quickly called them over to the car. I said that something dangerous was out in the woods and they quickly ran to the car and we sped away. While we were in the car, Rachel and I explained to them what had happened. All of a sudden, we halted. My friend who was driving had seen the exact same green eyes that I had seen in the forest by a tree that we had passed! To this day we still don't know what was out there.

The very next day, we called the police and they didn't find anything.

Submitted by Dean.

The Boneyard

On the edge of town there is a very old graveyard. It had a name at one point, but the marker has been worn down to such a degree that the name is now unreadable. Most of us just call it the bone yard. The graves are some of the oldest in America. Some of the tombs are falling apart and many of the graves are unattended. Sometimes you see a bouquet, wreath or some sort of remembrance, but not very often.

One day, I was walking home and happened to be walking past the graveyard. A man wearing a blue suit and tie, and old bell-bottoms was wandering through the graveyard. He had blue eyes, shaggy hair and sideburns. He looked like a caricature of the 70's. I watched him more surprised that someone was visiting the graveyard rather than by his appearance. He walked down a path, towards a grave and disappeared. Right in front of my eyes!

I have visited the graveyard since then to try and see him. I haven't seen him, but his grave is one of the newer ones. It does fit the time period. Did I see a man who died in the 1970? I think so.

Submitted by Bill

A Ghostly Gas Station

It was a Monday morning and it had snowed heavily overnight. I usually started work at 8:30 and it was already 8:15, so I would at least be 30 minutes late by the time I got to work. I noticed that I was low on gas so I stopped at the little town gas station on the corner of 138. As I sat there waiting for the attendant, I noticed that the town was curiously silent. I figured the lack of people driving around was due to the snow.

The older man who ran the station came out and I told him that I could only afford $5 in gas. He kindly offered to put $10 in the tank and when I got paid, I could come back and pay the remaining. I told him that it was very generous and that I would make stop in on Wednesday when I got paid. He said that was fine and I drove off.

The following Wednesday evening I stopped at the gas station to pay the balance. I walked in and there were two gentlemen standing there talking among themselves. I mentioned that I owed the older man money from him pumping gas on Monday morning. The two men looked at me like I had 3 heads. One of them said that it was impossible for me to have gotten any gas because the station was closed all day. I told him that I didn't have a receipt of any kind to prove it and then made a statement,

"Did it not snow on Monday?"

He said yes, but that wasn't why they were closed; they were closed because the older man had died on Sunday night. I said that it was impossible because he pumped my gas Monday morning and gave me $5 extra dollars worth. I also mentioned to the older man that I would be back on Wednesday to pay the balance due. The attendant checked the register and found a receipt from the older man, but it did not have a date on it. I told them that I wasn't crazy, and that if it hadn't been for him, I wouldn't have made it to work Monday morning.

I left the gas station knowing that I had been there Monday morning and that the ghost of this older man had pumped my gas.

Submitted by Anon.

Haunted Military Location

I work in the Public Affairs Office of the Armed Forces of the Philippines General Headquarters in Camp General Emilio Aguinaldo in Quezon City. Our office space and barracks are in the grandstands of this military base. Although the building is kept new by recent renovations and good maintenance, it is very much haunted. Since our office caters to the media and the military 24/7, we have people working night shifts. Although we sometimes feel and hear things during the day, it is during the night that weird stuff happens.

Personnel who work the night shift would sometimes hear the loose tiles of the floor near our boss's door clatter as if someone was walking circles or pacing at the dead of the night. No one is ever there if the duty personnel are brave enough to check and the sounds cease as soon as the lights are switched on. One duty person woke up to the sound of someone noisily typing at the desk computer of the research branch one midnight. Again, no one was there. Months later, I came to work in this office and the computer was issued to me. I shiver as I remember that I am writing this story using this same keyboard that he heard being used by invisible hands that night.

Our oldest staff member narrated that he almost had a heart attack when he was taking a bath at the office comfort room. He said that when he looked at himself at the mirror over the sink, he saw someone else staring back at him. He never described the face he saw to us because he could not remember it anymore. All he could say was that it was a young face.

One of our former officers, an Army Major, once said that he was spooked by shadows moving around near the supplies room. They would always be just in his peripheral vision. They disappeared whenever he tried to stare straight at them. Since we have no choice but to work with these ghosts, we just dismiss their presence as part of the experience of living in a military base. They might have been soldiers themselves who died fighting for our country or had loved their jobs so much they chose to remain soldiers even in the afterlife.

Submitted by Anon.

Ghosts On The Road

Given the amount of traffic and the number of accidents on roads it perhaps isn't surprising that roads are often the creepiest paces around. Here are a collection of submitted stories that involve weird happenings on our highways.

The Faceless Ghost

This incident happened to my daughter about 15 years ago, which would put her at the age of 13. Her father and she had been visiting friends for the day. They had left the friends' place at around eleven to head home. They were driving down a road that doesn't see much traffic that night. My daughter and her father were talking about a trip they were going to take the next day. All of a sudden, up the road in the headlight, there was a woman walking along side of the road. This was early September when the evenings get very cool. She had on shorts and was carrying something.

When the car was about 20 feet behind her, she stopped walking and turned around as if to see who or what was coming down the road. When the car got to about 10 to 12 feet from this woman, my daughter and her father were stunned to see that this lady had no face! She was also holding a blanket and there was movement under the blanket as if a baby was kicking. She was facing the vehicle as they passed her. Needless to say, my daughter and her father just looked at each other without saying a word. My daughter said her father was as white as a sheet. They never mentioned this incident for a long time. My daughter has many times tried to talk to her father about it, but he will change the subject.

Submitted by Mel.

The Ghost That Declined A Lift

My father used to tell me a story about an experience he had in the late 1950s, while on a sales trip through the hills of rural Pennsylvania. My father was travelling on a dirt road when he saw a rough looking man walking by the side of the road far off into the distance. He always said that his dirty faded blue clothes looked torn and he was stumbling, like he had either had too much to drink or had been in a fight. The closer he got to this man, the worse he began to feel for him and thought he would at least offer him a lift to the next town.

As he got closer, he saw that this man was all cut up and burned and wearing a blue uniform with a blue fedora with a yellow band. Then he noticed that the man was wearing a Civil War military uniform. My father went to pull over after passing him further up the road. He then sat there and waited for this person to come walking up to the car. Then he looked behind him and could see the man stumbling up behind the car so my father opened the side door for him and then sat and waited, but no one came to the door as he sat there. He looked behind him in the back window and the man had disappeared.

My father got out of his car and looked around, thinking the man may have tripped or fallen into the gutter. To his dismay, he could not find the man. My father just assumed for whatever reason, the man went off into the woods or something. Deciding to continue his journey, he got back into the car shut both doors and returned on his way. About three miles ahead there was a sign that read 'Gettysburg Battlefield.' My father said that when he saw that, it really creeped him out.

Submitted by Anon.

Ghostly Car in Detroit

Back in 1992, my wife was driving to work near Detroit, Michigan. On an isolated road in broad daylight, she came upon a car in front of her that was not moving. She slowed down and the car was engulfed in fog and completely disappeared right before her eyes. There was no side road or anywhere it could have gone. It vaporized completely. She cautiously drove through the area where the car had been and went to work. She was so shocked by the event that it was several days before she could speak of it to anyone. To this day she has no idea what went on in Detroit, Michigan.

Submitted by Anon.

The Ghostly Horse Rider

One late summer evening, when I was a boy, my family and cousins' family were walking back from a pub in the English Lake District to our campsite. It was dark. Very dark indeed. As we followed the winding country road up the hill towards our tents, we were chatting animatedly on various topics. It was then that my cousin heard the faint sound of a galloping horse from behind us.

"*Listen,*' she said, suddenly concerned that this horse rider might not see us in the road, *'let's move aside, a horse is coming.*'

We all stepped aside onto the grassy verges. Sure

enough, there was the sound of a horse galloping getting louder. We all waited. In the field to one side of the road, we all watched as a huge shadow passed by. It was dark, but the shadow was darker. A huge stallion and its rider. The rider was dressed flamboyantly in a large wide brimmed hat and strange clothes... although it was difficult to tell in the dark I will admit. We all watched mouths agape as this shadow horse rider rode by us not 20 meters away. The noise from its hooves was thunderous in the silence of the night. And then.... it was gone. The shadow, the sound. It simply disappeared.

We continued our walk home quietly. All contemplating the fact that, whatever we had seen and heard that night, it wasn't something normal ....a ghost rider in the night.

Submitted by G. Michael Vasey

My First Hand Experience of the Civil War

During a cross-country trip from Washington to Indiana, I had a strange experience at a Civil War battlefield. I have always been interested in the war, but I never had the chance to visit the battlefields before.

It was a balmy, warm day and I was looking

forward to walking across the battlefield and learning about the battle. We pulled over at the side of the road and started to walk towards the beginning of the battle route. It was a very bright day and there were other people around enjoying it. I didn't feel in anyway strange. As we climbed a large embankment though, I could hear talking. I put it down to other tourists. When we got to the top there were two men in full uniform talking with each other? I figured they were re-enactors. There is nothing strange about grown men in uniforms pretending to be Civil War soldiers.

Later we saw two riders on horseback, and we saw a bunch of other re-enactors marching back towards the top of the hill. We had a great time and I learned a lot about the battle. My wife and children and I finally reached the visitor site and I asked the lady there about the re-enactors. She looked puzzled and said,

"We don't have re-enactors here. It must have been kids,"

It wasn't kids! So what else could it have been? I believe we saw Civil War soldiers up close and personal. They didn't see us so were we ghosts in their timeline? Did my family and I slip back in time to the war?

Submitted by Bob

The Farmer's Daughter

I was Topeka Kansas born, but grew up in the Chicago suburbs. I went through the carpenters union apprentice program after high school. Returning to the Chicago area and after being a carpenter for a few years, I met what now would be called a cougar. This beautiful woman was from Ireland and though never a love relation, she owned a lot of property and had me renovate 6 or 8 places. She owned a bar and had apparently divorced 8 wealthy men. I only knew this as the patrons in her bar knew of at least 4, although when cleaning out a shed behind her house as requested, I threw out wedding pictures from 8 obviously wealthy guys she had married!

Anyway, she had me redo and make apartments out of a farmhouse in Downers Grove. It was by then surrounded by suburbs, but was the original farmhouse in that area before all the development. Joanie would come by once a week to pay me, but would only park in the driveway and refused to come in to view the work progress. I would complain, but she wrote the checks and so it went.

One day she came by to pay and I was like "*come in and look*" but she said "*I can't*" and she couldn't tell me why. Finally, after asking her many times, she broke down and told me the place was haunted and she didn't want any one to think she was crazy! I told her of my own recent ghost experiences in Minneapolis and then she opened up.

After her first divorce (I'm guessing about when I was born!), she got this house from her lawyer husband and brought her mother over from Ireland. She told me her mother would see a young girl follow her around the house, up and down the stairs. Well anyway, after a while, she told me she would be violently woken up in the middle of the night with a girls face and smoke inches from her face! This scared the crap out of her and she had a paranormal investigation done. They found out that the farm had burned down in the early 1800s and the farmer's young daughter had perished in the fire. They went on to say that in spite of the Catholic priests her mother and she had brought in to try to get rid of the spirit, that this girls' ghost continued trying to take over her body! Joanie never went back in that place and I know she told me the truth.

This was many years ago and if she were still alive she would be at least 80.

Submitted by Mark.

Demons and Evil Spirits

Some people have run ins with entities of the very darkest kind. However, the section starts with one that struck a real chord with me. In *My Haunted Life*, I tell the story about the green man. In fact, this is one of the earliest memories that I have as it occurred when I was just a small child. Lying in bed one night, I watched as a little green mad jumped out of the mirror on my cupboard, pointed a gun at me and pulled the trigger. There was a loud bang before my impish friend laughed and jumped out of my window. My parents, who were downstairs, heard the gunshot and came running up to find me in a state of shock and terror. I have to think, looking back, that perhaps what I saw was an elemental or nature spirit that decided to have a little fun with his victim. Perhaps he was a gnome or an elf?

Greedo

The story I want to tell to you is one that I will never forget as long as I live. Let me start by giving you a bit of background. The house that I grew up in was haunted and I still live there. It has got better, but there are still moments when I still get creeped out. This story is probably the best one.

I was 11-years old at the time. One night while sleeping, I was awakened by a presence in the room. I awoke without opening my eyes at first and was scared to do so because I knew something else was in the room with me. At the time, I was lying on my stomach with my face right at the edge of my bed. I finally got up enough courage to open my eyes, but when I did, I was terrified by what I saw. No more than a few inches from my face was the face of a miniature Greedo. For those of you who don't know who Greedo is, he was the alien from Star Wars that Hans Solo killed in the bar.

My mind raced to comprehend this strange green thing before me. It stood about three feet tall and I could make out its every feature; its big globe eyes, it's little ear things and it's long snouty nose, which was just inches from my face. I stared at it just long enough to try and comprehend what I was seeing and then I slammed my eyes shut. I prayed like never before for God to make it go away. I was sweating heavily and petrified with fear. Determined to get as far from this thing as possible, I ever so slowly inched myself toward the wall over the course of the next hour. I finally must have fallen back asleep because I remember having a dream that I woke up with my head now facing the wall and there were some pictures hanging crooked there. I reached up to straighten them and that's when Greedo grabbed me (in my dream).

I immediately woke up and it was still dark and I was now facing the wall as I had dreamed. I heard my dad getting ready for work and this gave me new courage to confront Greedo, if it was still in the room. I jumped up quickly on my bed and swung around to face it. It was gone. I immediately ran into my mom's room in hysterics and told her what had happened. I refused to sleep in my room for a full month after that.

Submitted by Cliff

Green Demon?

On the night before my sixth birthday, I woke up in the middle of the night because I had to go to the bathroom. On my upstairs floor, there was a hallway outside my room with my brother's bedroom to one side and my parent's room down at the bottom of the hall. Right next to their door was the staircase with a window halfway down to the ground floor. I always had the bad habit of looking over at the window and that night was no different. I saw a black creature standing in front of the window in a black robe with a hood over his face. The face looked green, but that could have been my imagination. The one thing I really remember is that it was grinning at me. Not a pleasant grin, but a really evil grin and I thought at the time that it was trying to lure me. I darted down into my parent's bedroom and woke them up. My dad went to see what he could see and saw nothing. I never saw it again. Could it have been a demon?

Submitted by Anon.

A Demon of a Party

I had a huge party to celebrate my 18th birthday and the morning after, the house was trashed. I got up early to clean up. After I'd finished cleaning, I ran to the shops. I came home and to my horror found the house completely trashed again. Angrily, I ran to get the phone as I thought my friends had come back and pulled the house apart again. Passing a mirror I noticed a face. A grinning demonic face grinning at me. I turned, ran out of the house and stayed at a friend's house until my parents came home the next day.

My friend woke me up the following morning and gave me the phone. My parents were home and found the TV smashed to pieces, their books ripped up and all the pictures looked burnt. Apparently, there were long, deep scratch marks on the walls of my bedroom and the dog wouldn't come out of the basement.

I still have no explanation for what happened, but I never had another party.

Submitted by Kate.

Red Demon

One day, during the summer vacation of my 3rd grade, my mom had gotten in touch with an old friend who was married to a pastor of a small community church. I was forced to go to church with my mom for a few weeks to 'reconnect with god'. I was a kid at the time that hated going to church and I found it boring, but soon I started to enjoy it. Within a couple weeks of going to church with my mom, a man started standing next to my bed to watch me sleep. I was a kid (maybe a tad smarter than my peers) and dismissed it as a figment of my imagination. I mean it seemed like a logical answer at the time. He was dark red, covered in horns, and had pitch black eyes. It would occasionally tilt its head to one side, but it never spoke.

I remember one night waking up to it just standing there watching me. Every night for a week or so I dismissed it as a hallucination until finally it got to me. I told my mom and her boyfriend. My mom was freaked out by how vividly I described it and how I showed her where it was. Her boyfriend took me into the kitchen and asked me to draw a picture while my mom went to call my pastor. I drew the picture and successfully freaked out her boyfriend. He asked me where it was again, but it had vanished.

My mom couldn't ring up the pastor, but managed to get a hold of my grandpa who is very religious. They gave me a prayer to say to get rid of it. (They automatically assumed it was a demon). The second that the words '*In the name of my lord and savior Jesus Christ Satan be gone*' left my mouth, he appeared and had an amused expression on his face. I swear it was smiling, but I will never really know because of all the horns and how scared I was to look at it. After saying it at least twenty times, he was gone and to this day I can't even recall his exact details or conjure it up in my mind. The picture I had drawn gave my Moms' boyfriend and I an uneasy feeling so we had him burn it.

Submitted by Anon.

The Demon in my Dreams
Some years ago, my family and I moved to a

house in Pittsburgh, PA. The previous owner had died suddenly and his family wanted to sell everything. So we moved into a house that was decorated in a very 1950's style. My room had an armchair, an old bed, an old stereo and a pile of dusty old books.

A few days later, bored, I went to my room and started to read one of the old books. It was about the paranormal. I soon discovered that all of the books were about the paranormal and inside one of them there was a newspaper cutting from the turn of the century. I discovered that the house that we had bought had once belonged to a priest who had, by all accounts, gone mad due to spending too much time on his own. I thought nothing of it. My father had told me that the President of a local bank had just owned the house so this man must have owned it many, many years ago.

Another week went by and I didn't think about it. But, one Sunday night I was trying to sleep and all I could think about was an old man scared and hiding in my room. A strange, scary creature with disconnected arms and legs was tormenting him. I was pretty creeped out, so I turned my light on and decided to do some reading. Of course, the only books in the room were the paranormal ones leftover from the homes' previous owner. I opened one of the books and saw a drawing. It was one of the creatures that I saw. Apparently, it was a demon of some kind and was well known. I was a young kid, I knew nothing about the paranormal and I hadn't seen that image before. Yet it still makes me wonder if I saw the past. Did that Priest come into contact with that demon I saw in my subconscious state?

Submitted by Anon

Just Downright Bizarre

Some of the stories submitted to the site are so strange and so weird that they defy belief and yet, I have had enough experiences of my own to know that they could well be truth and very real to those that experienced them. I indeed include one of my own about the witches daughter......

Sharing A Bed With A Ghost?

It was a December night and I couldn't fall asleep. My younger sister was already fast asleep in the other room. Suddenly, I felt cold hands tickle my feet and I said,

"*Angela!*" (Thinking it was my sister).

I put my feet quickly under the covers and turned over, not thinking anything more about it. Moments later, I felt something get into bed with me and they put their hand over my hand. I also felt their stomach going up and down against my back.

When I turned over to see what my sister was doing up, nothing was there. I freaked out and screamed. I woke up my whole family. My uncle came in my room and asked me what's the matter and I told him what happened. I slept with the lights on for the whole week. Then a couple nights ago, I was about to fall asleep and I heard my door open and little giggles, then someone tapping on my shoulder. No one was there a second time. I was so scared!

Submitted by Bobbi

My Girlfriend's Ghastly Friend

The absolute weirdest experience ever was when I was dating a girl while in grad school who admitted that she was kind of seeing someone else at the time, but he lived on the other side of the state. She told me that he and his previous girlfriend had been in a car accident the year before. One night, I looked out my window and there was something sitting on the balcony of my apartment, looking in at us. It was a woman, banged up and beaten up, with a huge gash in her neck. She just sat there, staring, and eventually disappeared while I blinked.

The next morning I asked the girl if she knew what the other guy's girlfriend had looked like, then described the thing that I'd seen the night before - she said that was exactly what she'd looked like, and that she'd bled to death in the accident from a neck wound. I broke up with her very shortly afterward - I didn't want another visit from whatever that was.

Submitted by Anon.

The Cursed Skull

A couple of my school friends found an ancient burial mound on the side of a hill, near Phoenix, that contained a silver-studded saddle and a skull. I was very wary about the find and warned the others that they'd better leave it alone. I just didn't feel it was right to mess around with a grave. One of my friends decided to take the skull and the saddle home with him. A couple of days later, one of my friends who had gone on the expedition got a call from the guy who took the artifacts asking him if he'd like the skull. Apparently his dad didn't want the grisly item in his house. You also have to remember that skulls were hot items back in the late 1950's for decoration and, of course, as candle holders.

My friend accepted the skull, collected it and after school he put it on top of the refrigerator in the kitchen and went to work at his part-time job. Later that night, his father came home from work and as he was getting ready to unlock the kitchen door, he heard a deep male voice talking from inside the house. He knew his son was at work, so he cautiously unlocked the door. When he stepped into the kitchen he still heard the voice and noticed the skull on top of the fridge. According to my friends' father, the skull was "lit up" with an inner glow and it was "talking," although apparently, he couldn't tell what it was saying. The next morning, my friends' father made us take it back to the desert and place it back in the mound it was stolen from.

Submitted by Anon.

The Visitor from Vietnam

A friend once told me a story about a college professor of his brothers who was a Nam Veteran. He explained that in a particular part of that godforsaken country, no man would enter. Well, a few of the soldiers did and they saw a creature there, which to this day, they cannot describe. The creature was about 10 yards away from the patrol, and in a blink of an eye, it was suddenly right in front of them, then suddenly standing behind them. After they returned home, this creature showed up at the professors' home in Maryland. It would physically make marks on his body and his wife's body. He contacted an old friend from the war who lived up in Canada, and he said it had visited his family, too. Apparently, all but one of the patrol have been visited by this creature.

Submitted by Anon.

Boy In The Closet

It was in 2008. I was working for a doctor as a certified nurses assistant and was also rooming in his home from which he had a private practice. One day, I was painting in the living room when I heard someone crying. The doctor came RUNNING down the hall at this crying noise to see if I was ok.

Later that evening, the doctor and his daughter went out to dinner. I was tired and decided that I would take a bath, but as I began to undress, I heard a lady crying. I opened the bathroom door, but no one was there. I went back into the bathroom and the same thing happened again, so I looked again and this time, I saw a lady with all white hair and she said, "*You can't leave him.*" To be honest, I thought that maybe I was just tired and so I finished my bath and went off to bed.

That night I had a dream of a boy climbing through the window in the sitting room and he said to me in the dream that "*everything was ok until he signed the paper.*" I told the doctor about the dream I had and he simply ignored me and changed the subject. Later in the week, I saw the boy again in a dream. This time the little boy came out of the closet and attacked me. I told the doctor about this and again he changed the subject. This happened a third time later that week. I must have fell asleep and when I did, I dreamed that I saw the boy come out of the closet and he said to me "*oh you are still here?*" The boy tried to put a pillow over my head, but I fought him off. I told the Doctor again what I had dreamed and again he tried to change the subject. I told him not this time and that I was leaving.

He called his daughter and told her what had happened and that I was leaving. She came over and I also told her what had happened She told me that the room I was in was her little brothers room. He had a brain thing going on and her dad had eventually pulled the plug on his life support. She showed me a picture of the boy and I thought I was going to fall out of my seat, as it was the boy in the closet in my dreams. The Doctor's daughter asked me not to leave because I could '*see*' and they needed my help. I told her that they needed JESUS and I left leaving my bible open. I never want to experience anything like that again.

Submitted by Linda.

The Witches' Daughter

Many, many years ago, I went on a school trip to SW England. One evening during the stay, there were some girls in the hotel of as similar age who had come for the weekly disco there. I was immediately attracted to one of them and over the course of the evening, did everything I could to hook up with her. I had some success and at sometime after midnight, I walked her home holding hands.

As we walked out of town down a dark country lane she began to become afraid and insisted that I leave her to walk the remaining half a mile or so on her own. She told me a rather strange story as we walked. She told me that her parents were witches and of the darker variety. She told me how she was forced to take part in rituals and was extremely scared. She told me that even now, I was in danger just by her being with me. I laughed at her creepy tale but stopped short when I saw the tears in her eyes. "*Go, quickly,*" she urged me, "*Before you have their attention.*" I have to admit that a touch of ice ran down my spine and after a quick hug, I left.

I arrived back at the hotel deeply perturbed by her story, but, as you do, I laughed it off and went to bed. At first, I was fine. However, as I lay on the point of sleep, a strange feeling came over me. As if I were being observed. Of course, I put this down to my imagination. I finally did fall asleep, but had very strange dreams and awoke in the later hours of the morning covered in sweat. It was very dark. In the corner of the room, I could swear there were two bright red eyes. I shut mine tight and willed it to go away, but when I opened my eyes again, there they were. Shaking I reached for the bedside light however, it did not work! There I was in sheer darkness with a pair of red eyes staring at me from the corner of the room and a growing air of malevolence in my small room. I was terrified. Who wouldn't be?

I began to pray silently. I invoked the forces of good to defend and protect me and more besides. The feeling of gloom and despair deepened. The eyes grew in intensity. I prayed more feverishly shivering in what was now a very cold room. Suddenly, the most amazing thing occurred. I saw a glow appear. Slowly it took on shape and solidity. What I saw defied any logic. It became a soldier in a bright blue uniform. It looked at me and the love emanating from his eyes was sufficient to calm me. It even smiled at me. In one movement, it raised its arm in a gesture that said 'begone' and that was it. The gloom lifted, the atmosphere turned into one of happiness, a fragrance passed through the room of roses and the first light of dawn peeked through the curtains. The eyes were gone and so was the soldier.

Submitted by G. Michael Vasey

A Jump Through Space?

I was taking a routine drive into town one morning. It's about two miles and it's a woody road that is spotted with a few houses. We often have fogs and mists that roll in, as there are several lakes in the area.

That morning a mist was rolling in, but I didn't take any notice. It was routine. I had gone half a block, pretty slowly, when I saw a light in the fog. I thought it was another car with its headlights on, but as I got closer I saw a market that I hadn't seen before. I pulled in to get my groceries and I was marveling at the fact that this new market had been built so quickly. I went inside and remarked about how quickly they had built the place. The manager looked at me and answered that the market had been there for forty years. I asked him where I was and he told me I was in a place that just happens to be on the other side of the country. I checked my watch and I'd left home about ten minutes ago. I have no idea what happened, but I do know that it took me **two days** to get home.

Submitted by Anon.

Unborn Child

When I was 12 weeks pregnant, I began to bleed and the pregnancy ended. I was devastated. Years later, I got pregnant again. I was about 5 months pregnant when my Husband and I started hearing running sounds upstairs from my bedroom to the landing and down the stairs. We could also hear the handrail move as it was directly next to the living room where we were sat. There was never anything there when we got up and looked.

This went on for a while and then baby things that I had bought went missing - toys etc. Then one day my neighbor came over to see me as I got out of my car and asked who was in the house as there were apparently children laughing and running up and down the stairs she said. This had gone on for some time she also told me. I explained that no one was home as I had just finished work. I went inside and all was quiet.
I then told my neighbor that I too had heard

noises many times. She said that she had got scared when she heard her son talking baby talk and found that her 1 year old son had got out of his cot and through the stair gate and gone down stairs one night. When she turned the light, on he looked as though he was holding someone's' hand, but as he turned to look at her, his hand dropped to his side. She told me that she was calling a medium in to see what was going on.

She knocked on my door a few weeks later to tell me what the medium had said. The medium had told her that there were children in the house. One child belonged to her and the other one belonged to me. He asked the children their names - the boy said nothing, but the girl said she belonged to me. She said her name was Rebecca and that she was 7 years old. I went cold at this news. I ran upstairs to get my old diary and went back to the day that I had lost my baby. We worked it out and indeed that child would have been 7 and there next to it I had named her Rebecca. You see I always knew it would be a girl. Not even my husband knew that I had written this information down in my diary and when he found out, he went as white as a sheet.

The medium told my neighbor that we could ask them to leave, but as they belong with us that was our job. I just asked them to be quiet and they were. When my son was born, the baby monitor picked up children chattering although I couldn't make out what they were saying, but it sounded as if they were playing. I heard this on a couple of occasions. Then I heard my bathroom door slam shut one day. I never heard them again after that until one day a few years back when she would have been 18 years old. I had the vacuum cleaner on and was thinking of her, which I often do, and in my mind I said "*I love you Becky*" and no word of a lie, I heard "*I love you too*" as if she was directly behind me. She hasn't gone. She is always here. I just hear her from time-to-time.

Submitted by Sue.

Strange Happenings in New England

This happened in New England in 1989. My daughter was almost four years old, and we had gone shopping for the day. I really didn't like to shop in the side of town that we were in. It was rundown and pretty dangerous there. As a child I had spent a lot of time in that area though we had lived near that shopping strip and my parents and I would shop there each week.

Most of the shops were empty by 1989 though. My daughter and I were walking down the side of the road - a roadside she had never been down before. To my utter surprise she asked, "*Can we go to the toy store after you've been shopping for food.*"

I knew for a fact that the toyshop had closed in that part of town several years before. I tried to explain that she had never been here before, but she turned to me and said "*We always went to the toyshop with you when you were a girl.*"

I was freaked out, but she was correct. I had gone to the toy store down the street all the time as a child with my mother. My daughter dragged me down the street and she then stopped in front of an empty shop and pointed. She was right. That's where Alan's Toys had been.

The next day, when I asked her about the experience, she told me that she had no idea how she knew. I don't know either.

Submitted by Debbie

The Ghost That Loved Me
One late evening I was lying in bed half-asleep

and half-awake waiting to go into a deep sleep. I'd been out with some friends drinking and had gotten home and gone straight to bed. It was unusual for me to be half-asleep and half-awake as normally a few drinks assure me of a full nights sleep. I was drifting off when I felt my wife get into bed next door to me. I heard her switch the light off and turn over. She was obviously interested in me that night so we made love and then I turned over and went straight to sleep. The following morning I woke up hung-over and she wasn't there and I remembered that she had been at a conference all weekend. So, whom the hell did I have sex with?

Submitted by Anon.

The Girl In The Mirror

I was young when I first started seeing ghosts. The first time was when I saw a woman wearing a white dress whose hair covered her whole face. I thought that would be the first and the last time, but I was wrong. That was only the first of my many encounters. I can feel them, and sometimes see them. But, I have never experienced talking to them (and I don't want to! That's too scary). Anyway, this one particular experience haunts me the most. I was still in college when this happened.

Our house is one of those many that survived WWII, yes it's ancient and the furniture is ancient too! I share a bed with my sister and one night while we were sleeping, I was awakened by a whisper. Someone was whispering to me! I was so scared, but I still opened my eyes and saw a woman's face near mine! I tried closing my eyes, but she whispered to me again, telling me that she wants to trade places with me! I tried to ignore her and silently prayed for this ghost to leave me alone. After sometime, she just disappeared. I prayed again and was able to sleep again.

The next morning, I told a friend who also has the ability to see ghosts about what happened to me the night before. She then accompanied me to our house when I went home. After doing some inspections, she found out that the ghost was from the ancient closet of my great grandmother. The woman's spirit was trapped in the mirror of that closet, and she really wanted to take over my body and to trap me in that mirror. My friend says that I was lucky she didn't succeed. After that, we switched rooms with my aunt. And I'm relieved that the ghost didn't bother me again, although I still feel her sometimes watching me.

Submitted by Anon.

About My Haunted Life Too Website

The website is located on the web at www.myhauntedlifetoo.com - it is a collection of your stories submitted by people just like you. Come over and visit us and leave your own story there too....

The site is hosted by me - G. Michael Vasey – and I am a collector of stories. We are partnered with Weird Darkness narrated by Darren Marlar – another avid collector of stories.

Everyone has a story.

http://www.myhauntedlifetoo.com

About G. Michael Vasey

G. Michael Vasey is a Yorkshire man and rabid Tigers (Hull City AFC) fan that has spent most of his adult life lost deep in Texas and more lately, in the Czech Republic. While lucky enough to write for a living as a leading analyst in the commodity trading and risk management industry, he surreptitiously writes strange poems and equally strange books and stories on the topics of metaphysics, occult and the paranormal on the side, hoping that one-day, someone might actually buy them.

After growing up experiencing ghosts, poltergeist and other strange and scary experiences, he developed an interest in magic and the esoteric. These days he fancies himself as a bit of a mystic and a magician to boot. Most of his inspiration for his scribbling comes from either meditation or occasionally, very loud heavy metal music.

He has appeared on radio shows such as Everyday Connection and X Radio with Rob McConnell to tell strange and scary stories. He has also been featured in Chat - Its Fate magazine and interviewed by Ghost Village and Novel Ideas amongst others.

He blogs addictively at garymvasey.com and he tweets micro thoughts at @gmvasey. He also reviews a lot of very weird books at strangebookreviews.com and collects true stories of the paranormal at www.yourhauntedlifetoo.com.

Other Books

- **Ghosts In The Machines** *(Kindle and audio book)*
- **How To Create Your Own Reality** *(Paperback and Kindle)*
- **God's Pretenders - Incredible Tales of Magic and Alchemy** *(Kindle)*
- **My Haunted Life - Extreme Edition** *(Paperback and Kindle)*
- **My Haunted Life 3** *(Kindle and eBook)*
- **My Haunted Life Too** *(Audio book, Kindle and ebook)*
- **My Haunted Life** *(Kindle, ebook and forthcoming audiobook)*
- **The Last Observer** *(Paperback, ebook and **Kindle**)*
- **The Mystical Hexagram** *(Paperback and*

Kindle)
- **Inner Journeys – Explorations of the Soul** *(Paperback and Kindle)*

Other Poetry Collections

- **Death On The Beach** *(Kindle)*
- **The Art of Science** *(Paperback and Kindle)*
- **Best Laid Plans and Other Strange Tails** *(Paperback and Kindle)*
- **Moon Whispers** *(Paperback and Kindle)*
- **Astral Messages** *(Paperback and Kindle)*
- **Poems for the Little Room** *(Paperback and Kindle)*
- **Weird Tales** *(Paperback and Kindle)*

All of G. Michael's Vasey's books can be obtained on any Amazon site and some can be found on other book sites such as Barnes & Noble, Apple and more.... He offers signed and dedicated paperbacks from his website at http://www.garymvasey.com

www.ingramcontent.com/pod-product-compliance
Lightning Source LLC
Chambersburg PA
CBHW071301040426
42444CB00009B/1826